UNDER THE TABLE AND DREAMING

Piano/Vocal arrangements by John Nicholas

Cover photography by: Stuart Dee
Photography © C. Taylor Crothers unless otherwise noted

 For a comprehensive listing of Cherry Lane Music's songbooks, sheet music, instructional materials, videos and more, check out our entire catalog on the Internet. Our home page address is: http://www.cherrylane.com

CONTENTS

Dave Matthews Band

Ants Marching • 9

What Would You Say • 17

The Best Of What's Around • 22

Satellite • 28

Typical Situation • 33

Dancing Nancies • 44

Rhyme & Reason • 55

Lover Lay Down • 64

Jimi Thing • 72

Warehouse • 79

Pay For What You Get • 90

34 • 99

DAVE MATTH

John Falls

There was a time when every rock 'n' roll movement sprung from the grass roots. While much has changed in the music industry over the years, a band working entirely on its own—outside the parameters of current trends—can generate the kind of organic electricity that marketers spend a fortune trying to create. Case in point: Charlottesville, Virginia's Dave Matthews Band.

In the four years since Matthews put together the genre-blending quintet, the band's charged live performances have consistently attracted packed clubs, theatres and arenas across the country. "It's been a very natural, very low-key progression," Dave says. "I don't feel like we've had this drastic, overnight success. It's basically been a matter of word-of-mouth—people liking what they've seen and bringing some friends with them the next time around."

Those die-hard fans have also snapped up copies of the band's self-released debut, *Remember Two Things* (over 250,000 copies sold since its fall 1993 release), on their Bama Rags Records label—a remarkable feat, considering the album was independently distributed. And while the band notes that the first release may have hinted at their potential, they are satisfied that their major-label debut, *Under The Table And Dreaming*—produced by Steve Lillywhite (U2, Talking Heads, Rolling Stones)—captures the nuances of their edgy musical amalgam and intricate interplay of the band's exceptional live persona. The critical praise for the album has since been exhaustive; *Rolling Stone* called it "one of the most ambitious releases" of 1994.

With singer/guitarist Matthews' expressive voice at the fore, the band—reedman LeRoi Moore, violinist Boyd Tinsley, bassist Stefan Lessard and drummer Carter Beauford—weaves a mesh of sounds that has been described as "unpeggable and totally addictive." Each member showcases a highly individual approach to his instrument, making the band a truly unique and eclectic ensemble.

"The way I look at it, we have five lead voices in this band," Dave continues. "I may be the first thing people notice, since I do the singing, but there are times when LeRoi's sax is the voice, and times when Boyd's violin is at the front. And in Carter and Stefan, we have something that goes far beyond a simple rhythm section. There are very few times when the audience has just one thing to listen to."

A glimpse at the 12 songs comprising *Under The Table And Dreaming* imparts the obvious: that the band is flourishing on its own musical terms, and in the process has veered far away from the susceptibility of new bands to being pigeonholed. On *Under The Table*, evocative melodies soar over compact grooves on the likes of "Satellite" and "Jimi Thing," while the band airs its more visceral nature on rockers like "Rhyme & Reason" and "What Would You Say." Such stylistic shifts occur within songs as well; the propulsive "Warehouse" boasts a richly-textured fusion-style break, while "Ants Marching" melds straight-up funk and a lively, high-lonesome bluegrass fiddle.

"In the beginning, I didn't have a fully formed idea of what I was going for," Dave admits. "I just set out to assemble my dream group of musicians—people I'd been listening to locally for years—and much to my surprise, they all agreed to join. And even after all this time, we still work the same way. There are no rules in this band, no one to say, 'Wait, you can't do that.'" With its absolute refusal to recognize borders and limitations, the Dave Matthews Band possesses the kind of musical chops and vision that the *San Francisco Chronicle* praised as "a means of expression free enough of cliché to be an authentic alternative."

Dave Matthews Band

DAVE SPEAKS OUT

The Best Of What's Around

Thanks to bad days and hard times, we notice the sweet nectar.

What Would You Say

A dog, a stuffed monkey and a television with 400 channels.

Satellite

We're awed by the wonders of technology. The accomplishments we've made to bring us closer together by plane, road or satellite are fantastic. What I fear most is that while we play with our toys and technologies, we forget from where our playfulness comes.

Rhyme & Reason

No rhyme . . .
no reason.

Typical Situation

Insert the last line of the
book *Animal Farm* and
attribute it to the author.

Dancing Nancies

What if you weren't
reading this?

Ants Marching

I love ants. We share a lot
with them . . . but they
are less talk.

LeRoi Moore

Carter Beauford

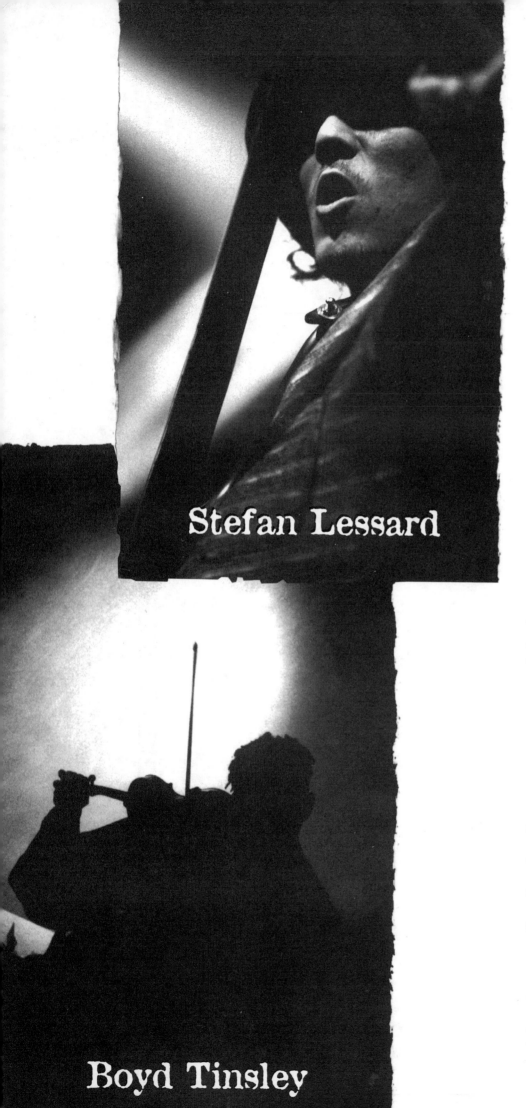

Stefan Lessard

Boyd Tinsley

Lover Lay Down

Careful with that word "love."

Jimi Thing

In England it's a condom.

Warehouse

Have you ever been in you[r] grandparents' attic?

Pay For What You Get

I spend a lot of time thinking about what I don't have and how I can get it. When I succeed in attaining it, often it comes with things I didn't expect.

#34

For Miguel Valdez.

Ants Marching

Words and Music by
David Matthews

The week ends, the week be-gins, she thinks. We look at each

oth - er, won-d'ring what the oth - er is think - ing.

But we nev - er say a thing and these crimes be - tween

us grow deep - er. *Instrumental solo ad lib*

and re-mem-bers be-ing—— small, play-ing un-der the

ta-ble and dream-ing. Take—— these—— chanc-es,————

place them in a—— box un-til—— a qui-et-er time. Lights——

—— down,— you up and die.——

(Sing 1st time only)
Instrumental solo ad lib

*Play 3 times

*On D. S. play 2 times.

12

red— and black an-ten-nae wav-ing. They all— do it the

same, they all— do it the same way,

— yeah. Can-dy man tempt-ing the thoughts of a

sweet tooth tor-tured, oh, by weight loss pro-gram, cut-ting the cor-ners,

Lights— down,— you up and die.——

What Would You Say

Words and Music by
David Matthews

Up and down the pup - pies' hair,___ fleas and ticks___ jump ev -
I was___ there when the bear___ ate his head, it thought___ it was a

To Coda

you may find— a life - time's passed— you by.——
morn-ing rise,

What— would you say?—— Don't drop the big—— one. If you a mon-key on a

well, don't cut my life - line. well. don't bite the mail-
string, If you a dog-gie on a chain,

man.— What— would you say?——

19

Ev-'ry— dog has its day, ev-'ry—— day has its way of be-ing for-

got-ten. Mom, it's my birth-day. Would you say,——— hey? (Now, what could you say?)———

——— What— would you say?———

Play 6 times

D.S. (lyric 2) al Coda

Coda

Tacet

What—— would you   say?——

21

The Best Of What's Around

Words and Music by
David Matthews

Moderate Rock

1. Hey,— my friend,— it seems— your eyes— are trou-bled.
2. *See additional lyrics*

Care to— share— your time— with— me?—

Would you say— you're feel - ing— low? And— so— a good—

noth - ing can be done,___ we'll make the best of what's a - round.___

Bridge

Turns out___ not where,___ but {1.3. who you're with___ that / 2. what you think___ a - that} a - real - ly mat -

ters,___ that a - real - ly mat - ters.___

24

Additional Lyrics

2. And if you hold on tight to what you think is your thing,
   You may find you're missing all the rest.
   Well, she run up into the light surprised.
   Her arms are open. Her mind's eye is...

2nd Chorus:
Seeing things from a better side than most can dream.
On a clearer road I feel, oh, you could say she's safe.
Whatever tears at her, whatever holds her down.
And if nothing can be done, she'll make the best of what's around. *(To Bridge)*

Satellite

Words and Music by
David Matthews

*R.H. tacet 1st time.

en.   Ev - 'ry - thing   good   needs   re   -   plac - ing.____

Look   up,   look down,____   all   a - round.   Hey,____   sat - el - lite.

Sat - el -

eyes._____

D.S. (lyric 1; take 2nd ending) al Coda

Sat - el -

Coda

N.C.

eyes._____

Typical Situation

Words and Music by
David Matthews

Ten fin - gers____ count - ing we have____ each.____

the big door o - pen. Ev - 'ry - one - 'll come a - round.

Why are you dif - f'rent? Why are you that way?

If you don't get in line, we'll lock you a - way.

It

ing.

1.3. It's a typ-i-cal sit-u-a-tion in these typ-i-cal times.

2. We can't do a thing a-bout it.

mp

Too man-y choic-es, hey, yeah.

Dancing Nancies

Words and Music by
David Matthews

Moderately

Could I have— been— a park - ing lot at - ten-

dant?———— Could I have— been———— a mil - lion-aire in Bel Air?—

—— Could I have— been———— lost some-where in Par - is?—

45

Moderately fast

46

an - y - one oth - er___ than___ me? And then I

look up at the sky. My mouth___ is o - pen___

___ wide. Lick___ and taste, what's___ the use in___ wor -

ry - ing?_____ What's the use in___ hur -

Bm   D

sing and___ dance,_____ la, la, la, hey,___

A   C#m/G# 4fr.

___ la,   la,   la,   hey,___ la,   la,   la,___

Bm   D

sing and___ dance. I'll___ play   for   you   to - night,___

A   C#m/G# 4fr.

___ the   thrill   of___ it___ all._____

53

Dark clouds may hang on me some-times

but I'll work it out. And I

look up at the sky.

D.S. al Coda II

Coda II

most be-come diz-

Repeat and fade

zy.
(Sing 1st time only)

Rhyme & Reason

Words and Music by
David Matthews

Moderate Rock

1. Oh, well,___ oh, well.___ So___ here we

2.3. *See additional lyrics*

Additional Lyrics

2. How long? I'm tied up, my mind in knots.
   My stomach reels in concern for what I might do or what I've done.
   It's got me living in fear.
   Well, I know these voices must be my soul.
   I've had enough, I've had enough of being alone.
   I've got no place to go. *(To Chorus)*

3. So young, here I am again, talking to myself.
   A TV blares. Oh, man.
   Oh, how I wish I didn't smoke or drink to reason with my head.
   But sometimes this thick confusion grows until I cannot bear it at all.
   Needle to the vein, needle to the vein.
   "Take this needle from my vein, my friend," I said. *(To Chorus)*

Lover Lay Down

Words and Music by
David Matthews

Spring, sweet rhy-thm, dance in— my head and slip in-to my— — lov-er's— hands. Kiss me,— won't you— kiss— me now— and—

Jimi Thing

Words and Music by
David Matthews

if you don't__ like__ it. Broth - er__ cha - os__ rule all__ a - bout.__ Well, some - time__ I walk__ there, yes,__ God knows__ some - time I take a bus__ there.__ Should - n't__ care, I should - n't care,__ be - reaved__ as I'm feel - in'.__

Warehouse

Words and Music by
David Matthews

Has me tied up in knots,_____ can't_____ test for a mo - ment.

Soon I'm go - in',_____

ooh, I'm slip - pin' slow a - way.

Hop - in' to find some - thing bet - ter_____ than I've

got in - side of here._____ And the ware - house slips

Bm

a - way._____
(Sing 1st time only)

Bm
Play 3 times

Hey! A

black cat chang - ing— col - ors.———— And we— can
black cat chang - ing— col - ors———— And we— can
black cat chang - ing— col - ors———— when it's not the

walk un - der——— lad - ders,——— and
walk un - der——— lad - ders,——— and
col - ors— that——— mat - ter,——— but that they

1.

swim as— the— tide——————— turns— you a - round and a - round,— a -
swim as— the— tide———————
all fade a - way,———————

Bm 2.

round. Hey! — choose to turn you.
— yeah, yeah, yeah. And

Pay For What You Get

Words and Music by
David Matthews

Suck the mar - row, drain— my soul.

Pay— your dues_____ and— your debts.—

Pay your re - spects.—— Ev - 'ry - bod - y tells— you, you—

—— pay for— what you— get.—— You pay—

You pay— for what— you get.— A - you pay— for what—

you get.—

Ev - 'ry-bod - y asks— me how— she's do -

ing. Is she real - ly all— she says?— } Ev - 'ry-bod - y asks—
ing. Has she real - ly lost— her...

Sur - prise,— sur - prise.— You pay—

—— for what— you get.— You pay— for what— you get.

D.S. al Coda

Ev - 'ry-bod - y - ask— me how— she's do -

96

#34

Music by David Matthews,
Leroi Moore, Carter Beauford
and Haines Fullerton

100

Cherry Lane
Music

• Quality In Printed Music •